REJC CHOICE

Skills To Achieve Success, Happiness and Fulfillment

Book # 1: The Basics Everyone Needs to Know

By Galit Goldfarb

© Copyright 2018 by Galit Goldfarb

Cover: Vikiana
Internal design, 2017, by Liv Gold.
Editor: Marlene Oulton, www.MarleneOulton.com

All rights reserved. No part of this book may be reproduced in any form or by electronic or mechanical means including information storage and retrieval systems except in the case of brief quotations embodied in critical articles or reviews- without permission in writing from the author, Galit Goldfarb.

This publication is designed to provide accurate and authoritative information in regard to the subject matter covered. It is sold with the understanding that the publisher is not engaged in rendering any professional service. If expert assistance is required, the services of a competent professional person should be sought.

All brand names and product names used in this book are trademarks, registered trademarks, or trade names of their respective holders. Galit

Goldfarb is not associated with any product or vendor in this book.

Table of Contents

Table of Contents 4
Dedication 6
Acknowledgements 7
CHAPTER 1 9
Introduction to Conscious Creating 9
The Rejoice Every Choice Principles 18
CHAPTER 2 20
Rejoice Every Choice Principle #1 for Creating Success, Happiness & Fulfillment 20
CHAPTER 3 31
Finding Your True Desires 31
CHAPTER 4 37
Rejoice Every Choice Principle #2 for Creating Success, Happiness & Fulfillment 37
CHAPTER 5 46
Rejoice Every Choice Principle #3 for Creating Success, Happiness & Fulfillment 46
CHAPTER 6 59
Clearing Self Limiting Beliefs 59
CHAPTER 7 70
Rejoice Every Choice Principle #4 for Creating Success, Happiness & Fulfillment 70
CHAPTER 8 85
A Daily 5 Minute Meditation Exercise 85
CHAPTER 9 92

Rejoice Every Choice Principle #5 for Creating
Success, Happiness & Fulfillment 92
CHAPTER 10 ....**97**
Rejoice Every Choice Principle #6 for Creating
Success, Happiness & Fulfillment 97
Closing Notes..**103**
Recommended Reading List 108
References: **113**

Dedication

I dedicate this book to my four daughters who have made me a better person and taught me how to reach my true potential. Raising them has taught me how to control my emotions, persist even when things get difficult and uncomfortable, how to be patient, and above all, they have taught me unconditional love. My daughters have also shown me that obstacles are really opportunities for growth, and that only my own attitude determines how situations I come across in my life are affected. I have learned the power of making successful choices in life and experiencing the consequences when my choices turned out to be mistakes. But most importantly, I've learned from my daughters that there is nothing we cannot achieve if we put our hearts and minds to the task.

I am who I am today thanks to them.

I also dedicate this book to all of you who are striving to make your life better. The happier we are individually, the closer we will be to creating a more peaceful and happier world for us all.

My website is dedicated to you! Check it out below:

www.GalitGoldfarb.com

Acknowledgements

The list of people I want to thank for the development of this book is exceptionally long and includes practically every person I have come across from the day I was born. Due to my contact with each and every person, my view of life has changed, my beliefs have changed, and my attitude towards life has changed. So I thank every person I know and have met in my life thus far.

Yet the people most responsible for this book becoming a reality include my husband, Amir, who has given me the space to do what I love and believe in. I can always count on him to be there by my side whenever I need him. He is a pillar of support for me through all of my ventures and I adore and love him from the bottom of my heart.

My truly remarkable father, who is an extremely talented musician and is still writing, composing, and playing music with his own band at the young age of 80 as of the writing of this book. He has been an inspiration to me and has proven that we can achieve whatever we want, at any age.

My mother, a talented business woman who inspires me greatly, has achieved much in her life, and has been a role model who has brought great insight into my life.

To my children, to whom I have dedicated this book, you have made me who I am today, through the unconditional love between us, and the ups and downs of life. I am who I am thanks to you.

I also want to thank Idan Reich for his integrity in telling me what I need to improve, and to Marlene Oulton who's brilliant work on creatively editing and refining the original manuscript has helped this series of books come alive.

CHAPTER 1

Introduction to Conscious Creating

"Men go to far greater lengths to avoid what they fear than to obtain what they desire."
— Dan Brown

    We each have the desire to be happier, but to be happy means many and different things to each of us. It is our choices in life which will determine how, when and whether we will reach our true desires or not.

    Life is sometimes filled with obstacles, and I have yet to meet the person whose life goes smoothly *all* of the time. People who have not given up on achieving their desires in life will be confronted with difficult choices at times. The formula I am introducing before you is designed to help you exactly at those times, showing you the path towards making successful choices in order to achieve all of your goals and desires in life.

We are each unique, but we all have the same basic needs and desires. We want to be happy and satisfied. In fact, the basis of each and every one of our choices and decisions is a basic belief that by making this choice or decision, we are creating a better, happier life for ourselves, either in the short or the long-term.

Throughout the years we have collected beliefs about ourselves and about life that we have come to accept as real. These beliefs sometimes distort our connection with our true inner being which is there to help guide us towards making successful choices that will truly create our happiness, and avoid ones that will not be beneficial for us.

In most countries, by law, from the age of 18 onwards, every person becomes responsible for their own life. When we reach that magical age, our thoughts, beliefs, behaviors and choices become 100% our own responsibility.

In my own personal life, from the time I became fully responsible for myself at the age of 18 up till the age of 28, when I made the shift, I had made all of the possible mistakes and bad choices that one could possibly make. Although by that time

I held two university degrees in the field of medicine, my studies never provided me with the information or insight of how to succeed in life. It was certainly not that I wasn't capable or not smart enough to do so. In fact, school testing indicated that my IQ was significantly above average. However, I didn't know or have the proper foundation for living a successful and fulfilling life and didn't understand how to make effective choices that would lead to my happiness, fulfillment, and prosperity. Truth be told, I ruined or wasted most of the good opportunities that came my way.

Through my bad choices and mistakes, my life became riddled with difficulties in every possible aspect. I was in a financial rut, my personal life was a disaster, and I was suffering from addictions, but this did not stop me from continuing to make further bad decisions. Only at the age of 29 after I had left my abusive marriage and was raising my two mentally handicapped daughters on my own with no money to put food on the table, suffering from bulimia, and still having court battles with my ex-husband over the custody of our daughters, did I finally reach the conclusion that I did not want my life to continue like this. I had to get my act together or else I would risk the possibility of losing custody over my daughters. This was something that I was not willing to accept.

Employing my knowledge and academic research capabilities I began studying the subject of success, happiness, and fulfillment in great depth. I then began transforming the knowledge I gained into practical steps to change my behavioral patterns and my life in general by making more successful choices, which eventually brought me to where I am now, living the life I'd always desired and enjoying happiness and personal fulfillment on every level independent on anything outside of myself.

As of writing this book, sixteen years have passed since the day I discovered these principles and when I look back at my life I can safely say that what seemed to be obstacles at the time, proved later to be opportunities for my growth, development, and personal fulfillment. These obstacles forced me to become a better, happier, and more successful human being.

I now understand that we need balance in all aspects of life in order to reach success, happiness, and fulfillment. All parts of our life need to work in harmony together in order for us to be headed on the right path towards fulfilling our true purpose for

which we came into this life. Balance in all of the important aspects of life includes:
- Peace of Mind
- Health and Energy
- Solid, Long-Lasting Relationships
- Financial Stability
- Fulfilling our Personal Unique Purpose.

Balance will only happen if we make the right choices in all aspects of life. Making the correct choices always stems from being honest and truthful with ourselves.

In this book I will introduce you to my formula which has helped me transform my life by making better, more successful choices in my life. By considering each of the principles before making any difficult decision, you will be happy with the consequences in your life and this will lead to your lasting success and personal fulfillment.

Life is like stretching a rubber band: if you take a pen and place a mark on the rubber band before you stretch it, you will notice that as you extend the band, the mark you made will move backwards. This is the same in life. If we are not moving forward and developing our performance in life, then we are actually moving backwards due to the expandability of our universe. Therefore the process of personal growth and continuous learning is an ongoing study that we should persist with throughout our lifetime. This perception of life allows us to also enjoy the WAY towards manifesting our goals and desires, rather than only expecting to enjoy the manifestation of the desires themselves. The WAY towards achieving our goals is why we came here. This is the creation process with all its glory, and this is thoroughly based on the choices we are making every single moment of every single day.

For over 400 years scientists thought that once we reached adulthood our brains were fixed entities that could not grow or further develop, and that the intelligence we were born with and learned throughout our early childhood years is how we would remain for the rest of our lives. Therefore there was no need to mentally train our brain.

But today, science understands the plasticity of our brains, and that through our experiences we can form new brain cells (neurogenesis), as well as build new connections between brain cells (neurons) which allows us to acquire new skills, behaviors, and to improve ourselves at any age. In fact, we are physically capable of modifying our brain to become better at doing anything that we focus our attention upon. So if you are often behaving in an unproductive mode, this will become your default behavior pattern. By training yourself to make better, more conscious choices in life, and by focusing your attention on the end product of how you want your life to be, you are actually changing your brain default activity mode to one that will support you in life.

"Do not spoil what you have by desiring what you have not; remember that what you now have, was once among the things you only hoped for."
— Epicurus

A feeling of dissatisfaction with your current situation is actually a very good sign. It means that it is time to improve your current lifestyle or change it for something better for yourself because you have evolved and developed. Therefore feeling dissatisfied is actually a positive sign. It means that it is time to align yourself with a new and expanded version of yourself in order to fully realize your highest potential. It means that there are a whole host of new opportunities awaiting you. You just have to align your energy, beliefs and behaviors, or in other words, your choices with your new and expanded version in order to enjoy these new opportunities that await you.

People who restrain these feelings of dissatisfaction once they have them so that they will not need to leave their comfort zone are not really living life. J.K. Rowling, the British novelist best known as the author of the Harry Potter series, which became the number one bestselling book series in history, [1] expressed it precisely when she said:

"It is impossible to live without failing at something, unless you live so cautiously that you might as well not have lived at all, in which case you have failed by default."

In this book, part 1 of a 5 book series, I will introduce to you the formula for making successful choices so that you Rejoice Every Choice. This very practical formula will help you excel in choosing the right path for yourself towards achieving the lofty goal of Creating a Successful & Happy Life.

The strategy I use is simple, practical, and will help you select the right course of action at the right time to create exactly what you want in life.

It's like driving a car: when you want to get somewhere, you first have to learn to drive, get a permit, then you have to choose your destination and learn the way to get there. If you do not know how to drive the car or if you do not know where you want to go or follow the directions to get there, the likelihood of you arriving at your desired destination is slim.

We are all part of the creative process and if you want to consciously create and reach your desires, you will have to take an active role by making successful choices that will get you there. The Rejoice Every Choice series of books will teach you how to do this easily, with less stress, less unhappiness and less frustrations.

The Rejoice Every Choice Principles

Our lives are the sum of the choices we make. By using this formula you will understand whether your choices are pointing you in the right direction towards a happy, purposeful life filled with fulfillment and well-being, or not.

Are you ready to make your dreams come true?

Let's begin.

The **Rejoice Every Choice Principles** to consider before making any choice are as follows:

I. Value
II. Love
III. Belief
IV. Action
V. Focus
VI. Future

All of these principles must be present in any positive, life promoting choice. They must cumulatively exist if you are to be happy and fulfilled with the path you are taking.

Understanding the deep meaning of each principle will also help you to understand yourself better.

In this book we shall delve into each principle so as to understand its importance. In the following books in this series we will learn to apply the Rejoice Every Choice strategy to different aspects of life that you may wish to improve. When you use this method for making successful choices in each specific aspect of life, you will increase your feelings of success dramatically in that area of your life.

Each of the **Rejoice Every Choice Principles** in this strategy consists of a set of questions that by answering them you will help yourself make successful choices in life. Your responses will help you determine whether your choice is the right one for you, and whether it will enhance your life or not.

Now let's go into depth of the first of the **Rejoice Every Choice Principles** in the strategy.

CHAPTER 2

Rejoice Every Choice Principle #1 for Creating Success, Happiness & Fulfillment

Value

"A man who dares to waste one hour of time has not discovered the value of life."
— Charles Darwin

The first set of questions to ask yourself:

- *"Will this choice give me Value?"*
- *"Will others gain value from this choice of mine?"*
- *"Will this choice make me happy?"*

The first principle towards making successful choices is knowing and understanding whether the choice you are making comes from ***YOUR*** true desire, or is it rather a desire you have formed to conform with society or with someone else's wishes. In order to allow alignment with your true desires you must first examine whether your choice will add value to ***your*** life. It is good to pinpoint the value you expect to get once your choice will manifest in your life.

Reexamine the choice and ask yourself "Will this choice I am making really add value to my personal life or not once it manifests in my life?

A survey from Salary.com revealed that 61.5 percent of Americans are not happy with their job. (2) Only 38.5 percent of the 2,000 American workers surveyed said they were "personally fulfilled by the work they do". Another joint study from PARADE magazine and Yahoo!-Finance with 26,000 American participants found that about 60% would choose a different career if they felt they could. (3) It is very difficult to be satisfied in life if the majority of the hours you spend during the day, you are doing something which does not satisfy you. Therefore, for your happiness and fulfillment, you must consider whether this choice will add value to ***YOUR*** life or not.

When I went to study medicine, it seemed like a perfect thing for me to do. I was very interested in helping others, and I had already 5 years of university study behind me in this field as well as 4 diplomas in the alternative medicine field. When I began my studies, however, I had a growing feeling that this was not right for me. I loved studying the science behind medicine, and loved helping others, but by not truly being able to find a solution to their problems, and rather going about only covering up their symptoms, I did not feel satisfied. I decided to leave my studies and go on to finish a masters degree program in medical science instead.

Of course the years of studies themselves added value to my life, however, I felt that working as a medical doctor would not allow me to really help others as I wished to help them. I felt that my calling was elsewhere where I could add more value to others by looking at the deep core of peoples problems and finding deep rooted solutions instead.

It is just as important for you to obtain value from all of your choices as it is important for you to provide value to others from your choices in order to feel fulfilled, happy and successful in any and all fields of life.

Once you know that indeed your choice will add the value you wish for into your life, then it is time to ask yourself the question "Will this choice add value to my close family and friends and to others as well as to future generations?"

The story of Sara Blakely is an excellent example to this. Blakely is an American businesswoman and founder of Spanx, the multi-million-dollar hosiery company.(4) In 2012 Blakely entered the Forbes list as the world's youngest self-made female billionaire at the age of 41. As of 2017, she is listed 16th on the list of America's self made women by Forbes.(5) Blakely came up with idea for Spanx when she was 27 years old. The idea for the special hosiery came to her through her own personal need. Blakely was working at Danka, an office supply company where she sold fax machines door-to-door. While on the job, she was forced to wear pantyhose in the hot Floridian climate, Blakeley disliked the appearance of the seamed foot while wearing open-toed shoes, but liked the way that the control-top model eliminated panty lines and made her body appear firmer. One evening Blakely was invited to a private party where she experimented by cutting off the feet of her pantyhose while wearing them under a new pair of slacks. She found that the pantyhose continuously rolled up her legs, but she also achieved the desired result of appearing firmer and without panty lines. At age 27, Blakely relocated to Atlanta, Georgia, US, and while still working at Danka, spent the next two years and her savings researching and developing her hosiery idea. (6)

In November 2000, Oprah Winfrey named Spanx a "Favourite Product," leading to a significant rise in popularity and sales, as well as Blakely's resignation from Danka. Spanx achieved $4 million in sales in its first year and $10 million in sales in its second year.(6)

If your choice will make you **happier**, then this choice will also add value to you, your family and friends. When you are feeling happy, then you affect positively all those whom surround you and you enhance their lives just by the fact that you are happier. This is certainly an addition of value to their lives.

If this choice will not exactly make you happier, but you feel that it is a good thing to do, and that it will add value to those around you more then it will add to your own personal happiness, I truly recommend you think through your desire once more.

Your desires should make **_you_** happier, and should allow **_you_** to enjoy life more. This is why we are here. This is the difference between someone who does something for the benefit of others but does not really enjoy doing it, to someone whom is doing something they love and is also a benefit to others; the second person whom is doing it with passion will succeed much more than the first person.

Just because you feel that your choice is the "right" thing to do, if it won't make you happier, then please reconsider going after it. You will be a great success in something only if you truly have the passion for it and it will definitely make you happier and enrich your own personal life in the process. This is the reason we are living life. To find our joy and let it flow from us and positively affect others.

A person considering creating a family and bearing children and changing their life from very career oriented to a stay-at-home parent, because that is what they were raised to believe this the right way to live, but will not enjoy being, playing or caring for the children very much, is best either to reconsider this choice of creating a family with children or to plan to have a solid income in place to help employ a very passionate caretaker whom will help care for the needs of the children.

A teenager getting ready to go to college and chooses their degree title to conform with their parents' desires, while it is really not their own personal desire to study that specific subject, will not be enjoying their time at university and will certainly not become one of the more successful graduates who combine passion with skill together.

A person who may have many skills in their chosen profession but does not enjoy it any longer and does not receive enough value from the job, should perhaps choose a different direction and not necessarily climb the corporate ladder and desire a better position in their company.

The value you are adding must first and foremost be to yourself. If you know that this particular choice will add value to your life, and to those close to you, then you have begun the path to successfully making the right choice.

Your choices should also consider adding value for future generations. It is very important to consider the impact your choices will have on your future generations if you want to be happy in the long run. Try to avoid making choices that may have a negative effect on your personal future and those of your future generations; these choices will not add value to your life in the long run and may lead to much suffering for you and those close to you.

When I was 21 years old, I really wanted to get married and start a family of my own after having my own family fall apart as a child. However, it seemed to me as if my father was not happy with any man I would bring home to meet him. I really wanted to please my father with my chosen spouse, but found no man that my father would approve of. I was actually choosing my husband by what would make my father happy rather than what would make me happy. Later, I understood that this was a very distorted way of thinking, and proved to be a very bad choice on my part.

I decided to marry my first cousin whom I believed my father would approve of. Due to the familial closeness between my husband and I, we were first cousins after all, our two daughters were both born with an autosomal recessive disorder that led them both to suffer from severe mental retardation. The likelihood of having both of my daughters, whom were born one-and-a-half years apart, suffer from mental retardation is almost non existent if I were to marry someone who is not my relative. But by marrying my first cousin, this likelihood rose to 25% for each child, and this happened twice for us! This is certainly an example of when our choices do not add value to our future generations.

By examining the value principle for all of your choices, including choices you have already made, you can also determine if you are currently in the right position for yourself at this moment or if you should consider change.

If you are still gaining value from where you are today, for example, being in a specific relationship, job, or any chosen path. Keep following the ***Rejoice Every Choice*** strategy to help you determine whether you should remain in your current situation and improve it, or leave it altogether to follow a new venture. Sometimes staying in a relationship, job, career may be something you can benefit more from than if you leave it altogether. You will get a clearer answer to your questions as to which path you should follow as you continue with the ***Rejoice Every Choice*** strategy.

Muhammed Ali said it well when he said: "Service to others is the rent you pay for your room here on earth".

Adding value to yourself and others is the first principle towards making successful choices.

For those of you whom are still not clear on your goals and desires, go to the next chapter to help you with this process.

If you feel you know your desires and goals precisely, you may skip the next chapter and go directly to the next principle in the ***Rejoice Every Choice*** strategy to making successful choices in life, Love.

CHAPTER 3

Finding Your True Desires

What are your Goals and Ideals that you want to live by? Have you thought about this? This chapter will help you pave the path to living your life to the fullest.

Complete the short questions below to help you come up with your own truthful answers from your inner being.

Before you find your goals in life, you must first get to know your personal ideals and understand where you want to be. After knowing these answers you can find your goals and follow them persistently until you reach your ideal life.

Now is the time that to get to know yourself more intimately. Perhaps you think you know yourself, but sometimes through living life, we forget who we really are and what we really want. Sometimes we are so overwhelmed with responsibilities and so overwhelmed with decisions and problems that we forget our responsibility to ourselves. Your responsibility to yourself is to live life to the fullest, to enjoy life and to follow your true desires and this means that you should first find out what that means for you.

Following is a short exercise that always works for me. It helps to bring out secrets that are hidden within your subconscious mind that, at times, you may not be aware of. I call this exercise "The Exercise Of Truth". This exercise will help you to find your truth of what it means for you to live life to the fullest. This exercise will surely help you to find your goals for life.

Now first get a pen and paper or a word processor. Find a quiet place where you can complete the exercise (which will take approximately 25 minutes) without being disturbed by anyone or anything.

Ready to begin <u>The Exercise Of Truth</u>?

Answer the following questions as fast as you can, do not edit any spelling or grammar mistakes while you are answering the questions, this is not important. Just let your truth flow out of you without allowing your conscious mind to intervene in the process.

Answer each of the two next questions in 30 seconds each.
Write down the first thing that enters your mind, without thinking. Just go with the flow.

1. What does your ideal relationship look like?

2. What are the five most prominent characteristics of your ideal partner?

Take a few minutes break and continue

Answer the next three questions as fast as you can write the first thing that enters your mind:
In your ideal life:

1. Where do you live, which town, country?
2. What car do you own?
3. What type of house do you live in and where is it located physically?

Take a break for a few minutes and continue to answer the next four questions.

Take 30 seconds maximum to answer each of the following questions:
1. What does your ideal employment look like?

2. With whom do you work?
3. How much income a month do you need to be happy?
4. Ideally, How would you like to achieve this income?

Take a short break and continue.

Answer the first thing that enters your mind to the following three questions:
1. What is your ideal weight?
2. When are you happiest?
3. What do you need to do with your body to know that you are on the path to lasting health?

Take a short break and answer the next four questions in 30 seconds each:
1. What will make you feel fulfilled?
2. Do you want children? How many?
3. What do you like to do for others?
4. How do you see yourself doing this for others?

Take a short break and answer the following question in one minute:
1. How do you behave in your ideal life?

Take a short break and answer the next question in 3 minutes:

1. How does your ideal life look like? Describe your picture to me.

Now you have your answer to what living life to the fullest means to you. Now all you need to do is to make the right choices to get you there. Continue the path outlined in the ***Rejoice Every Choice*** strategy and you will be well on your way to making the right choices that will lead you toward achieving all of your dreams and desires.

CHAPTER 4

Rejoice Every Choice Principle #2 for Creating Success, Happiness & Fulfillment

Love

"Sometimes the heart sees what is invisible to the eye."
- H. Jackson Brown, Jr.

The second set of questions to ask yourself:

- *"Does this choice originate from true love to myself and others?"*

- *"Do I really Love this choice?"*

Once you ask these two questions, the answers you give yourself will provide you with answers as to whether or not you are headed in the right direction towards achieving your desires. All external desires are born from an internal desire that we feel we are deprived of. You will only reach your true internal goals that you are feeling lack from if your choices are based on value and love.

Firstly, determine if you will truly love this choice once it has manifested. Once you will have it, will you love having it? The answer to this is not so obvious for all of our desires. If a choice you make will manifest and you will not love enjoying its final manifestation with all its glory, then this is a choice worth second thoughts.

Secondly, it is important to determine whether your choice originates from true love to yourself, and not from a position of pleasing others or from fear of something else manifesting. If the choice originates from pure true love to yourself, then, and only then the manifestation of this choice will make you truly happier. If the choice does not originate from a place of true love to yourself, then you should rethink this desire. You should go about aligning yourself with only things that you feel love for. The things you feel love for will make you feel good, and only the things that make you feel good in life are important to your experience if you wish to live life to the fullest.

I will give an example from Oprah Winfrey's life. When she was in her 20's, she was working as a reporter in Chicago and although her salary was considered very high in comparison to other people her age living in her area, she was not happy. All of her family and friends were telling her that she hit the jackpot with her reporting job but she felt that she was not going with her truth even though her job seemed glamorous to others. She kept asking herself what she really wanted to do, until one day she was invited by her boss to do a talk show instead of reporting. Oprah claimed that it was immediate love. At that moment she claimed that knew that that this is what she loved doing and this is what she really wanted to do. At the time Phil Donahue ran the first talk show format that included audience participation.(6) The show was a phenomenon in Chicago and Chicago was considered a racist city, which led to many limiting beliefs about her ability to succeed there being a black woman. However, Oprah chose to go with her love and started to host WLS-TV's low-rated half-hour morning talk show, *AM Chicago*. The first episode aired on January 2, 1984. Within months after Winfrey took over, the show went from last place in the ratings to overtaking *The Phil Donahue Show* as the highest rated talk show in Chicago! Two years later, the show was renamed *The Oprah Winfrey Show*, which brought in double Donahue's national audience, displacing Donahue as the number-one daytime talk show in America. *The*

Oprah Winfrey Show, aired nationally for 25 seasons from 1986 to 2011 and remains the highest-rated talk show in American television history. (7)

The show received 47 Daytime Emmy Awards before Winfrey decided to stop submitting it for consideration in 2000. (8) Oprah was ranked the richest African-American of the 20th century, (9) the greatest black philanthropist in American history,(10-11) and is currently North America's only black billionaire.(12) She is also considered to be the most influential woman in the world.(13-14) In 2013, she was awarded the Presidential Medal of Freedom by President Barack Obama (15) and an honorary doctorate degree from Harvard.(16)

It is so important to go with what you truly love in order to reach the success and fulfillment you desire in any field.

The love step of the ***Rejoice Every Choice*** strategy towards making successful choices in life is different from the value principle. Value can be something external, having value only for your ego, without having any benefit for your inner being. Moreover, a choice which provides you with value may not necessarily be something you will love to have. I will give a materialistic example here: My dream was to own a yacht. After I had started to make some money from real estate, I decided that I was going to fulfill my dream of owning a yacht. I certainly believed that once I had this yacht it would certainly add value to my life. I would imagine my husband and I going off on romantic sails in the yacht, having my kids enjoy swimming at sea and enjoying being at one with nature. I believed that being out at sea was like being in constant meditation. Then one day my whole family came over from abroad for the holidays and I suggested that we rent a yacht for the day and enjoy swimming at sea. I was sure that we would all really enjoy the experience. We rented a beautiful yacht and shortly after leaving the port, things did not feel for me as I had expected them to feel. I was not happy at all. I started feeling seasick and so did almost everyone else on board except for my mother and my father's wife, even though the sea was fairly quiet. The captain suggested that we jump into the water and this would help us feel better, so we took him up on his suggestion and my brothers, father and sister and I all jumped into the water. One brother began vomiting at sea but the rest of us felt slightly better until we were back on board the yacht. Once on deck all of us started to vomit non stop. It was a nightmare. We had to stop the cruise after less than an hour.

When we finally arrived back at the port, I thanked the captain and told him that he had just spared me a lot of money today because I now decided that I was not going to buy a yacht any more.

This is what I mean by love. When your choice manifests, will you love having it and will it make you feel good? These are the important answers to determine at this stage.

A UK study done by the Office of National Statistics in 2013, surveyed over 150,000 UK citizens about their well being. (17) Due to the size of the study, it allowed the researchers to have a finely detailed analysis as to what affects peoples' experience of life. The results show that material living standards are insufficient to fully capture people's experience of their life, meaning that money doesn't always equal happiness. (17) Having good relationships, a good quality of life, enjoying the place where one works and the environment where one brings up their children has a much higher impact on the personal happiness and fulfillment level of people. Therefore, at the end of the day, remaining true to yourself by choosing fulfilling choices for yourself will have the greatest impact on the quality of your life.

It is your happiness that counts; and doing what gives you value and that which you love and do with passion will place you where you truly want to be in life.

Another thing to consider is whether your choice originates from fear or love. If a desire originates from fear, manifestation of it may lead to much chaos in your life, just as my choice of marrying my cousin lead to much chaos in my life. The choice of marrying my cousin came more from fear than it did from love. I feared being alone without a family, and I feared displeasing my father. Choosing from love to yourself first, and then to others will certainly lead to better choice-making on your behalf, and these choices will allow you to live your life in more peace.

If you are in a current position where you are unsure and uncertain as to which path to follow in the near future, consider whether you truly love what you are currently doing and whether you truly love with whom you currently are. If you found that you do have value from your relationship, job, position, place of residence etc, and you find that you do love the person, job, place, then you can certainly think about remaining in the position you are currently at and find ways to improve on it so that you will continue to experience personal growth and development. Keep following the principles noted ahead and your answer will become clearer towards the end.

A feeling of love towards something is an indicator that you can still gain happiness by following this choice.

For a happy, fulfilled life, it is always best to make choices that originate from pure love to yourself and to others.

CHAPTER 5

Rejoice Every Choice Principle #3 for Creating Success, Happiness & Fulfillment

Belief

"One person with a belief is equal to ninety-nine who only have interests."
-John Stuart Mill

The third set of questions to ask Yourself: "Do I really believe in this choice?", "Do I really believe this choice is right for me?", "Do I believe I can do this/ achieve this/ make it work?"

This is the third principle towards making successful choices in life. Once you have determined that your choice will add value to yours and others' lives and you will love having it in your life once it has manifested, and that the choice originates from true love to yourself; the next step is determining how much you believe in its manifestation and how much you believe in your ability to manifest it and how much you believe in this choice, period.

Change from without comes from change from within. Our choices have the power to change our lives in the exact proportion that we believe in our choices and in ourselves.

All of our choices come from our beliefs about the situation and about ourselves. What we believe we are able to accomplish, is what we ***will*** accomplish; no more and no less.

Look at famous people whom were rejected for those precise things they are famous for. The one thing that allowed these people to continue on their path was their belief in themselves. Walt Disney was fired from the Kansas City Star because his editor felt he "lacked imagination and had no good ideas," Oprah Winfrey was fired from her job as a television anchor for getting "too emotionally invested in her stories," Thomas Edison's teachers told him he was "too stupid to learn anything," and the list goes on.

Our beliefs arise from the thoughts that we choose to entertain about ourselves.

We will always behave and perform in the exact way that we believe we can and will perform in any given situation, and this will lead to our choices. We tend to choose choices within what we perceive as being within our capabilities.

For example, If you have a low self esteem, you will believe you can only have a certain type of partner, and this is the partner you will tend to pair up with. People with a low self esteem usually pair with a partner with a low self esteem, however, one partner will try to use the other partners' low self esteem to raise their own low self esteem which lowers the other partners self esteem even more. What tends to happen is the relationship disintegrates, and both partners are left with an even lower self esteem than they began with.

Our beliefs present the boundaries of our abilities. You need to believe in your ability to create your desire and only then will your choices match your true worth, and this begins by first making a decision to change your perspective and start to believe.

In order for your true choices to manifest in your world, you may want to believe that you have help in manifesting whatever it is that you desire, that you are not alone to deal with all of the details of the manifesting process. There is guidance from above if we are willing to listen to the subtle signs from the universe.

Belief is the basis for any manifestation. It is not necessary to understand the exact mechanism by which things will manifest nor do we need to deal with all of the details of the manifestation. We do not need to have all of the answers. However, we do need to believe that we have the ability to create whatever it is we want by simply believing in ourselves, our creative abilities and guidance from above.

It is like turning on the light, when you lift the light switch, you expect the light to turn on. You do not need to understand everything, or even anything about electricity for the light to turn on, you just need to raise the switch. The light will not turn on better or stronger for those who are more electrically knowledgable, and the light will not switch on less for those who have no knowledge whatsoever about electricity. The light will turn on equally to all those willing to raise the switch.

If you can see other people whom have created what you desire to have in your life, there is no reason under the sun that you should not be able to create the same for yourself if this is your desire.

We are all born unintelligent, and through time, learning, experiences and our environment, we create connections between neurons (brain cells) in our brain.
The human brain consists of about 100 billion neurons, They transmit information to other parts of the body through both chemical signals, and also electrical signals. (18)
Different neuron connections bring on different emotions. Apparently, the brain creates our mind and our mind creates our brain.

New technologies of filming and scanning the brain in the last two decades have proven that the brain is like plastic, and can easily adapt to change.(19) The brain can learn new skills and create new connections and activity patterns. Our brain is dynamic and constantly changing throughout our lives through experiences we have, through suggestions we have chosen to accept as real which form our beliefs, and through mental control if we choose to use it.

Wherever we choose to place our attention upon, the thoughts that occupy our mind most of the time will become habitual, our second nature. (20) There is a saying by neuroscientists that goes: Neurons that fire together, wire together. The brain cells that tend to fire in a specific pattern together, tend to choose that pattern of firing together on a regular basis and become default thought patterns. (21) These specific connections become stronger and more efficient through constant usage while others become weaker. (22) Therefore, the more we feel a certain emotion, the more it becomes our second nature to feel that way.

By mastering our thoughts, we are actually training our mind. By training our mind, we can modify our brain cell firing connections to ones that help us achieve more happiness and fulfillment in life, instead of defaulting on brain cell firing connections that make us feel miserable just because they have become our second nature.

We can reprogram our mind to create better, more supportive brain cell firing connections, in fact, there is strong evidence that shows that any talent can be created through training of the mind. You can be anything you desire to be through training of your mind. (23)

So, we can certainly also modify our brain connections to those that will allow us to gain control of our emotions just as we can learn any new sport or new skill.

In fact, whenever we focus upon something most of the time, we are physically modifying our brain to become better at doing it, so if we are unhappy most of the time, this will be our default brain activity. By practicing self awareness, examining our belief and thought patterns, we ***can*** greatly affect our level of success, fulfillment and happiness in our life by affecting our brain's default firing activity.

Belief is made up of thoughts which come from faith in ourselves and in the process. In the same way that limiting beliefs stop us from getting what we desire, positive beliefs and faith will assure that we do get what we desire through determination and persistence.

Our thoughts, which make up our beliefs, will always determine the outcome of our life, because whatever we believe we can achieve, we will achieve. The science behind this fact lies in our subconscious mind.

The Subconscious mind makes up around 90% of our thinking power. (24) Our conscious mind holds thoughts that we choose and thoughts of our desires. When we are thinking consciously, we are moving towards our goals, however, we are usually only conscious less than 10% of our time. The rest of the time, most of the population work through their programmed subconscious mind, and therefore people tend to make the same mistakes over and over again by making the same kind of bad choices. (24-25)

The subconscious mind collects information and retrieves this information when it is required. The thoughts used by the subconscious mind are habitual thoughts that we have allowed to be programmed into our mind. We have accepted certain thoughts as being real, because either they were planted in our mind during childhood, when we did not have the skills to choose which thoughts to accept, and which to reject, or through personal experiences or through other people, whom we admired or looked up upon.

Belief is the basis to all of the actions you will take in life, and the actions you will take in life will form the outcomes of your life. The only thing holding you back from achieving your true potential is the limiting beliefs you may be holding, because they block the three characteristics needed to create the life of our dreams:

1. A high self esteem
2. A belief in yourself and your abilities
3. Persistence to go about our goals until you reach them

Believing we are worthy of receiving our desires is the basis of any step towards achieving these desires. If we are all creative beings, creating our lives one thought and choice at a time, then we are all capable of achieving anything our thoughts can imagine, and since we each have different desires in life, we are each in the perfect setting for us to create the perfect reality for ourselves. Once we understand that the setting, however unsettling it may seem at the moment, is the perfect setting for us to go about achieving our desires, then we have accomplished this stage of the manifestation formula.

Henry Ford put it well when he said: "Whether you think you can, or you think you can't, you are right".

Without believing in ourselves, we cannot achieve anything. Without believing in our ability to choose the best for ourselves, we will not manifest the best for ourselves. Nothing is ever a mistake, everything we experience is another step forward towards the path of our enlightenment.

It is so important to take full control of our thoughts and beliefs and the method to do this best is to watch carefully over the beliefs we have about ourselves and the thoughts we allow to enter our mind and control our lives. Since what we believe to be true about ourselves, will eventually become true, it is important to determine the ideal you and to focus on that ideal rather then focusing on reality as it is at the moment. Paint a picture in your mind of the ideal you, how do you feel, think and behave, what are your characteristics? Write these down before you. If you can imagine an ideal version of yourself, this means that it is possible for you to reach this ideal version. Research in the field of quantum physics has shown that reality is a figment of our imagination.

We are creators creating with our minds. Anything we can imagine under the sun, we can conceive into our reality. Once you believe this, you will pose less resistance to it and allow the good things that you desire for yourself to enter your life with more ease and comfort.

Does your choice fit into the ideal version that you have of yourself?

Can you picture yourself in the full possession of this desire?

If you can do this, and you also believe in your worthiness to have this desire. Then you have passed this principle and can move on to the next principle. However, if you can visualize yourself having all that you desire in the version of the ideal you but do not believe you can do, get or achieve it, then it's time to remove some limiting beliefs that are holding you back. You can do this by reading the next chapter. If you do not feel that self limiting beliefs are hindering your advancement and holding you back, you can skip the next chapter directly to the next principle in the Rejoice Every Choice strategy to making successful choices in life, Action.

Due to the importance of the Belief principle behind all of your choices, and making successful choices has very much to do with how much you believe in yourself, I have created a whole course precisely on this subject due to the fact that this is the basis towards achieving any and all of your desires. In this course I teach you all of the skills and techniques I have used to transform my own life, when my life was falling apart. This course will allow you to change your viewpoint and gain mental control and allow for changes to ease into your life with harmony and peace. You are welcome to join my course at the following address:

https://www.theguerrilladiet.com/the-magic-8-step-formula

CHAPTER 6

Clearing Self Limiting Beliefs

"I would never die for my beliefs because they might be wrong."
-Bertrand Russel

We each hold a set of limiting beliefs. For some of us this set can be very large. These limiting beliefs may encompass every field of our lives. It is important to clear self limiting beliefs as much as possible so that you can become the best version of yourself and reach your true potential of lasting fulfillment and happiness. But first, *what* are these limiting beliefs and *where* do they come from?

A limiting belief is anything that limits your abilities of achieving anything you desire in this world. If you consider that we all come from one same source, then, we can conclude that we all share the attributes of that source.

We are always creating, because this is our essence. We may be creating unconsciously, or consciously, the choice is always ours. Whatever is filling up our lives today, we have created. Whether we create positive life conditions or negative ones is all dependent on the amount of joy and connectedness we feel to our true self, an unlimited creator.

Because we have created, through our choices, and are therefore responsible for everything in our lives after we reach adulthood, we each have the ability to overcome any difficulty and even make the best of any situation we are confronted with.

There are things in life that we cannot change or control, for example, the death of a loved one, a handicap that we have, a weather catastrophe that hit our country, etc. However, we always have a choice in determining how we perceive things and how we react to these situations.

On the other hand, situations that we can always change and recreate into a better version include our financial situation, no matter where we are today, no matter where we live today. The same goes for our health, peace of mind, our relationships and our family life. We are where we are today because of the choices we have made up to this point. These choices where made from our personal beliefs of who we were, what we were capable of and how much connection we felt with our true self, at the time we created. Once we start choosing better choices for ourselves, ones that provide us with true joy, choices that add value to the world and to ourselves, choices that come from love, belief and happiness, we will start to fly and create the most amazing life for ourselves.

Now you may be asking yourself: What is holding me back from achieving my desires if I can create anything under the sun? The answer lies in your limiting beliefs that you have gathered through the years from sources that you respected and admired, from caretakers, parents, teachers and friends. We have also made some up for ourselves following life experiences that we experienced. We see the world as limited, when in fact it is absolutely unlimited. Even if we are physically limited, we are still unlimited with what we can achieve, within the boundaries we have created for ourselves. But with the use of some imagination, that we were given in plentitude for the creative purpose, we can clear self limiting beliefs and free ourselves to our true potential.

We were given imagination so that we can create, and we CAN create EVERYTHING that we can imagine in our minds, we just have to go about it in a methodological manner, and with persistence, determination and belief, we will reach our goals and desires.

Lets take for example Albert Einstein, a German-born theoretical physicist and philosopher of science who developed the general theory of relativity, one of the two pillars of modern physics (along with quantum mechanics). Einstein won the Nobel Prize in theoretic physics but he was not always considered to be smart. At the age of 16, Einstein sat the entrance examinations for the Swiss Federal Polytechnic in Zürich, Switzerland but failed to reach the required standard in the general part of the examination,(26) although he did obtain exceptional grades in physics and mathematics. (27) Instead, he attended the Argovian Cantonal School in Aarau, Switzerland, to complete his secondary schooling.

Einstein did not give up and continued to push himself forward and although he was only 17 years old, he enrolled himself in a four-year mathematics and physics teaching diploma program at the Zürich Polytechnic. In 1905 Einstein published four groundbreaking papers, on the photoelectric effect,

Brownian motion, special relativity, and the equivalence of mass and energy, which were to bring him to the notice of the academic world and allow him to become a household name in everything that involves intelligence. (28-30)

In 1921, Einstein was awarded the Nobel Prize in Physics for his explanation of the photoelectric effect, as relativity was considered still somewhat controversial.

In 1939, Einstein and Szilárd a Hungarian physicist attempted to alert Washington of ongoing Nazi atomic bomb research. The group's warnings were discounted.(31) Einstein and Szilárd wrote a letter to President Franklin D. Roosevelt to alert him of the possibility of the Nazi's developing the bomb. The letter also recommended that the US government pay attention to and become directly involved in uranium research and associated chain reaction research. The letter was believed to be the key stimulus for the US adoption of serious investigations into nuclear weapons on the eve of the US entry into World War II".(32) President Roosevelt could not take the risk of allowing Hitler to possess atomic bombs first. As a result of Einstein's letter and his meetings with Roosevelt, the US entered the "race" to develop the bomb, drawing on its "immense material, financial, and scientific resources" to initiate the Manhattan Project. The US became the only country to successfully develop an atomic bomb during World War II.

Einstein was even offered the position of President of Israel, a mostly ceremonial post in 1952.(33) However, Einstein declined, and wrote in his response that he was "deeply moved", and "at once saddened and ashamed" that he could not accept it. (34)

The sum of all of our beliefs make up who we are today. We will always act, behave and become in accordance with our beliefs. Only we are forming the boundaries of our abilities.

We have beliefs that we have collected or developed for every aspect of our lives, from how good a cook we are to how much money we can earn.
That is why we call these "limiting beliefs". They put us into a certain frame of mind from which we find it difficult to leave its boundaries.
Well, its time to clear these self limiting beliefs and leave these boundaries behind. Its time to start living the life of your full potential.

Now lets start an exercise that will help you remove your own personal limiting beliefs:

STEP 1: Visualize:
Think about the IDEAL version of yourself.
What are you doing in your ideal form?
How do you feel ideally?
Where are you living ideally?
With whom?
Visualize your ideal YOU and the ideal life for YOU?

Please use the gift of imagination you were given. Use it to create a vision of the ideal you now. Please create the vision of the ideal you based on your own terms. Do not think about the ideal you in terms of your mother, father, teacher, or neighbor. Think about the ideal you that comes from your soul. What are your real desires? What is YOUR TRUTH about your ideal self?

Beforehand I asked you to imagine the ideal version of yourself using your imagination, now it's time to put it to writing.
Please take a pen and paper.

Write down your truth of what your ideal is in terms of:

1. Relationships including both family relations and romantic relations
2. Living accommodations
3. Health
4. Financial circumstance
5. Most importantly, write down your ideal YOU characteristics, what are the characteristics you hold in the Ideal version you have of yourself?

This 5th principle is usually the hardest for us to put on paper, because we may still be stuck in terms of what we can and can't be, so to help you fill this last step out, I want you to write down a list of 5 people you really admire and consider as WINNERS. The list can have people from any walks of life. The list can include people whom you know personally or those you have do not know personally, this doesn't matter.

For each person on your list, write down the 5 characteristics they have that you truly respect and admire. Write down why you consider them as winners.

Name of Person You Admire / Respect	First Ideal Characteristic	Second Ideal Characteristic	Third Ideal Characteristic	Fourth Ideal Characteristic	Fifth Ideal Characteristic
1					
2					
3					
4					
5					

Now you have before you a list of 25 characteristics that you consider as ideal, although your list maybe be shorter because there may be overlap for some of these characteristics.

For every ideal characteristic that you found, write down:

I, (enter your name), **am**, (write down the characteristic that belongs to the ideal you).

The point of this exercise is to form a new picture of yourself, and to create a new belief system that will not be ruled by limiting beliefs. The ideal you is what you consider as being a winner, and you deserve to be that ideal person you want to be. Not only do you deserve to be that person, you can absolutely be that person. Remember that most of us are only using 1-5% of our brains' potential! The reason is not because we can't use more of our brains potential, it is because we are the only ones whom are sabotaging our chances of using any more of our potential through the limitations we have created for ourselves. If you can imagine something in your mind, then you can certainly create that something.

The only way to change your life is to change your beliefs about everything that you believe is limited. It's about time, for you, and for those around you, and for the world that you start projecting the ideal you.

The next step is to print out the list of the ideal you in a small square note that will fit as a sticker on the back of your mobile phone. Laminate the list and buy a double sided tape and stick it on the back of your phone, or just leave it in your wallet, and have a look at this list as often as you can throughout the day.

This will slowly diffuse into your subconscious mind which will allow it to become your reality. You will gradually release the old, limited beliefs you are holding of yourself, and will allow space for the new, unlimited, amazing you to finally shine through.

CHAPTER 7

Rejoice Every Choice Principle #4 for Creating Success, Happiness & Fulfillment

"When it is obvious that the goals cannot be reached, don't adjust the goals, adjust the action steps."

-Confucius

Action

The fourth set of questions to ask yourself:

"What choices can I make to forward my desire?", "What are the choices I can make to advance the manifestation of my desire?"

Now that you believe you will and can give value to yourself and to others through your choice, and your choice comes from true love to yourself and to others, and you truly believe that this choice is right for you and you believe you can achieve it; it is time to choose the right action steps towards achieving your goal.

The action principle involves taking both proper physical and mental actions towards achieving your goal.

<u>The physical action principle may involve some of the following:</u>
- Choose to study whatever you need to know in order to accomplish your goal.
- Choose to initiate small changes that are required to bring you closer to accomplishing your goal.
- Make a plan and start taking any small steps you need in the direction of achieving your goal, in the end they will amount to much progress.
- Keep yourself going in the right direction of achieving your goal but if you see any signs that show that your actions are not supportive of

your endeavor, if you do not see any progress, be flexible enough to slightly change direction of your actions, and you WILL eventually reach your desires.
- Choose to take physical action by doing things that make you feel good in the process.

Physical actions are very important since they will be moving you forwards and allowing you to become more knowledgable in your field and what you need in order to reach the manifestation of your desire. As I mentioned in the chapter on belief, you do not need to have all of the answers. You just need to keep moving forward in the direction of your desires. Do whatever you can do, and do not even consider what you can't do at this stage, it is irrelevant for manifesting your desire.

The place you are currently at, is the perfect place for YOU to start to achieve your desire. It does not matter how far away from your desire you may be at the moment, you are in the best pace for YOU to start the process of creation right where you are standing today. Remember, it is a process, and you need to change in the process to become a better version of yourself in order to reach your desire.

The mental action principle is just as important as physical actions in the manifestation process, because only what you believe, you will conceive. It is important to keep your beliefs in the process and in yourself high, and this is not always easy.

The mental action principle involves: Mainly choosing the right thoughts and learning to master your mind.

In his book "*As A Man Thinketh*", James Allen gives an analogy of how our mind is likened to a garden:

In our mind we have two spheres of brain activity, the conscious mind and the subconscious mind.

The conscious mind is like the farmer who chooses which seeds to plant in the soil, as well as being responsible for caring for the soil.

The subconscious mind is the soil. It will always bring to life whatever is planted in it.

The soil never cares what is planted in it by the farmer. The farmer will always reap whatever he has sown.

The seeds planted by the farmer are the thoughts and beliefs that we, the farmer (the conscious mind) choose to allow to be grown in our soil (which is the subconscious mind).

Just as the soil welcomes any seeds planted by anyone in it and will reap whatever is planted, the subconscious mind is open to suggestions from anywhere and anyone. We can use our conscious mind (the farmer) to choose to control which suggestions (seeds) are accepted (planted) in our subconscious mind (the soil) and which are not.

Through faith, repetition and expectation we can imprint on the subconscious mind the exact things that we desire to have in our life.

We can do this through auto-suggestion instead of allowing for hetero-suggestions (given by others not necessarily in our favor) to lead our actions.

Auto-Suggestion was discovered by Émile Coué de la Châtaigneraie, a French psychologist and pharmacist in the beginning of the 20th century. It is a psychological technique which uses "Mantra-Like"conscious suggestion to be absorbed by the subconscious mind. The method uses routine repetition of specific suggestions, at the beginning and end of each day. Coué explains in his book, "Self Mastery Through Consciousness Autosuggestion", written in 1920, how autosuggestion relies on the idea that "*any idea exclusively occupying the mind turns into reality, although only to the extent that the idea is within the realm of possibility.*" For instance, a person without hands will not be able to make them grow back. However, if a person firmly believes that his or her asthma is disappearing, then this may actually happen, as far as the body is actually able physically to overcome or control the illness. On the other hand, thinking negatively about the illness (ex. *"I am not feeling well"*) will encourage both mind and body to accept this thought. Likewise, when someone cannot remember a name, they will probably not be able to recall it as long as they hold onto this idea (i.e. *"I can't remember"*) in their mind. Coué realized that it is better to focus on and imagine the desired, positive results (i.e. *"I feel healthy and energetic"* and *"I can remember clearly"*).

The best time to auto-suggest to our subconscious mind is at night, before bed or early in the morning upon waking because this is when our five senses are least alert and the two spheres of our mind activity are closest to each other.

Our subconscious mind never sleeps, it is awake 24 hours a day and therefore is always working on making our thoughts our reality 24/7.

Our subconscious mind will bring to fruition whatever we believe to be true by expecting that which we believe to be true to appear and choosing unconscious choices that help make our beliefs become our reality. Indeed we are unconsciously choosing through habit over 90% of the time that we are awake.

No willpower is strong enough to overcome what the subconscious mind perceives to be true and this is the reason why most people find it so difficult or downright impossible to stick to new habits. The subconscious mind is stronger than willpower and it must slowly be reprogrammed to allow any real change to occur in our lives.

Repetition of chosen thoughts will help us to reprogram our subconscious mind to get us the results that we desire to have in our life.

For the mental action principle for making successful choices, we must master **The Law of Cause and Effect**:

Every cause leads to a specific effect. Our thoughts are always the causes to everything we have in our life because they form our beliefs, which form our expectations, which are the foundation of our choices, behaviors and actions.

Our actions represent our life.

- Remember that nothing is ever imposed upon you, everything is created from within. We have the creative power to produce everything we desire, one thought at a time, with

persistence and with faith and belief in ourselves and in the process.
- Details are not important, the big picture is. Keep the big picture of what you want in your mind and the details will fill themselves in.
- Know that your default system is progressive, you will always be moving forward towards achieving your desires all the time; your primary job is to stop interfering with the progressive process by ceasing to hold onto your limiting beliefs in the focus of your mind. Remember that you don't have to know the precise way towards achieving your goals or desires, you don't have to understand the exact process and all of the details involved. Your job is to remain faithful to the larger picture. Remove all beliefs that are limiting you, keep hopes and beliefs in yourself and the process high. This is your mental work.
- Motivate yourself to keep going in any way you can. Listen to motivational videos, read true and similar biographies of people who have succeeded in your field, and mainly keep yourself in contact with people who are supportive of you and your ideas and goals.
- Let nothing trouble you, not your circumstances at the moment and not what you

fear may happen in the future. Keep your mind only on what you desire to achieve and on what makes you feel good, and what will lead to joy for you, for those close to you and the world.
- It is also very important to ignore whatever does not feel good. Point your mind towards only what feels good and take both mental and physical action from this mindset.

Abraham Lincoln is an excellent example of someone who learned to master his own mind. He was going through grave difficulties in life: He failed at business when he and a partner bought a small general store on credit in New Salem, Illinois. Although the economy was booming in the region, the business struggled and Lincoln eventually sold his share. At the time, Lincoln's fiancee, whom he loved dearly, died at the age of 22 most likely of typhoid fever. (35) and he lost three of his four children all under the age of 18 to various diseases which led him to suffer from deep clinical depression. (36)

However, Lincoln decided to continue to follow his dream and began his political career with his first campaign for the Illinois General Assembly. Although he lacked an education, powerful acquaintances, and money, he attained local popularity and found that he could draw large crowds to listen to his speeches in New Salem. Lincoln decided to take physical action and to get an education. He taught himself law by reading law books voraciously and by reading Blackstone's *Commentaries on the Laws of England.*

In 1836 he achieved this goal and was Admitted to the bar examination, (37) and moved to Springfield, Illinois, where he began to practice law. Lincoln became an able and successful lawyer with a reputation as a formidable adversary during cross-examinations and closing arguments. (38) However, his dream was in politics. Lincoln, now with an education and some powerful acquaintances that he met during law studies, got voted for congress. However, Lincoln's dream was the presidency. He was defeated in 8 elections due to his stance against slavery and abolitionism but he didn't give up. He was persistent, and he believed in himself and kept on going, taking the proper actions, through all of his adversities, to reach his goal of becoming President of the United States.

Finally, on November 6, 1860, Lincoln was elected the 16th president of the United States. He was the first president ever from the Republican Party.(39) He took America through the Civil War which had its origin on the issue of slavery, especially the extension of slavery into the western territories. (40) Lincoln closely supervised the war effort where he made major decisions on Union war strategy. During the war, Lincoln wrote the Emancipation Proclamation in 1863 whereby he used the Army to protect escaped slaves, encouraging the border states to outlaw slavery, and helped push through Congress the Thirteenth Amendment to the United States Constitution, which permanently outlawed slavery.

Lincoln has since been consistently ranked both by scholars, and the public as one of the greatest US presidents and the most loved president of all time. (41-42)

Learning to master your mind and take full control over your beliefs by taking full control over your thoughts is the most important step towards achieving the success, fulfillment and happiness you desire in any field.

This has been proven by scientists in the fields of Physics and Psychology. A famous study that has been done a number of times includes the use of a 0 or 1 Random Number Generator. This is a computational device designed to generate a random sequence of 0's and 1's, that lack any pattern. It has been found that a person with an intention of getting a specific number (either more 0's or more 1's) while starting the generator, did tend to get a significantly higher amount of this number rather than the other number. The overall results could not be attributed to chance, or selective reporting problems, or variations in design quality. These studies clearly indicate that there are ways in which mind and matter interact that support the possibility of the effect of human intention and expectation on the results received by the generator. (43-46) Quantum mechanics, the study of the tiniest particles of the universe, suggest that objects are not be completely independent of consciousness or observation. (47-50) Some theorists argue that rather than being paradoxical or contrary to theoretical expectation, some form of mental influence on physical objects should in fact be expected. (51) We do have influence on our life through our thoughts, therefore careful monitoring of our thoughts is critical to achieving anything desirable in life.

A very simple technique to help master your thoughts includes meditation. Neuroscientists from Bangor University in Wales have discovered that meditation can stimulate significant increases in activity in several parts of the left prefrontal cortex, the area of the brain associated with positive feelings including happiness, enthusiasm, joy and self-control. (52) Meditation has been found to actually promote neuroplasticity, the brain's ability to change, structurally and functionally, at any age, on the basis of environmental input by encouraging new connections between neurons. (53) Research by University of Wisconsin led by Richard Davidson has shown that experienced meditators exhibit high levels of gamma wave activity and display an ability to not get stuck on a particular stimulus, meaning that experienced meditators are more able to control their thoughts and reactiveness to life situations. (54) A study on American men and women who meditated a mere 40 minutes a day showed that they had thicker cortical walls than non-meditators, meaning that their brains were aging at a slower rate. Cortical thickness is also associated with decision making, attention and memory. (55) Meditation has also been shown to protect telomeres, the protective caps at the end of our chromosomes which are the new frontier of anti-aging science. Longer telomeres mean that you're also likely to live longer. Research done in the University of California by Shamatha Davis has shown that meditators have significantly higher telomerase activity that non-meditators. (56)

Animals whom have telomeres which do not degrade may in fact live forever. Research suggests that lobsters do not slow down, weaken, or lose fertility with age, and that older lobsters may, in fact, be more fertile than younger lobsters due to telomerase, an enzyme that repairs the telomeres, long repetitive sections of DNA sequences at the ends of chromosomes. The enzyme telomerase is found in vertebrates during embryonic stages but is generally absent in adult stages of life.(57) However, unlike most vertebrates, lobsters express telomerase as adults through most of their tissues, which has been suggested to be the reason for their longevity. (58-60)

Meditation also produces a calming effect in the amygdala, the part of the brain that acts as a trigger for fear and anger. (61)

Meditation allows us to go within ourselves and use our intuition to pick up on our true desires. Meditation also allows our conscious mind to give productive and positive orders to our subconscious mind for it to bring about in our life. Therefore, I have created a 5 minute meditation to help you keep your beliefs in the process high. This early morning meditation can help you start the day in tune with your desires. This early morning meditation helps you to create and stick to those beliefs that you will need in order to carry out your desires to fruition.

In the next chapter (#8) you will learn a 5 minute meditation that will help you attune your mind to conscious creating of the things you desire.

The next principle of the Rejoice Every Choice strategy to making successful choices follows in chapter 9 where you will learn the fourth principle of the strategy, Focus.

CHAPTER 8

A Daily 5 Minute Meditation Exercise

"If we know the divine art of concentration, if we know the divine art of meditation, if we know the divine art of contemplation, easily and consciously we can unite the inner and outer world"
-Sri Chanmoy

This daily 5 minute meditation exercise is one that has helped me tap into the method that helps people achieve their dreams.
This 5 minute meditation exercise, when done twice daily, will assure you achieve your goals, like it has done for me.

The reason why this meditation works is because it slowly convinces the creator inside each and every one of us to believe that what we want is already ours and all we need to do now is to allow it to enter into our lives.

As I mentioned previously, our subconscious mind is the creator within us. It accepts what it believes to be real and makes it our reality, because habitual thoughts bring about those things that we expect into our lives.

By constant repetition of certain actions, that I will tell you all about in a minute, your subconscious mind will accept and believe that what you want and desire for yourself is already yours, and when you act and believe that something is yours, you become satisfied and happy and these are states that allow the good that you want to enter into your life.

This change of belief will lead to a change in your reality, and miracles will start to happen. In fact, whatever you can imagine in your mind, you can physically create. No picture that has come vividly into your mind is unattainable, because if your mind can picture it, you can create it in your physical reality, period.

The Meditation:
You can create your own style for this meditation if you please. The important thing is consistency, persistence, acceptance, understanding and believing in the process. The precise method by which this happens is not important to understand, just as it is not important to understand how your smart phone works to make it do the things you want.

The 5 minute meditation exercise goes like this:
Lie on your back, or sit in a comfortable position, eyes closed and eyes focused on the middle of your forehead.

Make cups with your hands and clap them together to make a soft cupping noise. This helps summon the unlimited energy that surrounds you.

Repeat the following words throughout the whole meditation: "It has already happened" or "I already own it," which ever sequence you most relate to.

Meditate on each area of your life for about one minute, if you are unbalanced in one particular area, focus on it for a bit longer.

Begin by touching or circulating above specific areas of your body that are weak due to anything, be it dis-ease or dis-comfort, and say repeatedly "I Am

Healed... it's already happened". I do this repeatedly for 1-5 minutes.

Then I touch my heart and continue the chanting" I have a Wonderful Relationship...it already happened". I do this repeatedly for 1-5 minutes.

Then I touch my pockets and say: "I have Much Abundance...it's already happened". I do this repeatedly for 1-5 minutes.

Then I touch my head and say "I am Extremely Happy...it's already happened". I do this repeatedly for 1-5 minutes.

While I am chanting, I visualize images of the end results as I would like it to be (what I desire, the end product).

Then ground the energy off of your fingers by making a flicking action with your fingers towards the ground. This helps to ground any negativity you take away from yourself.

Continue chanting "It has already happened"

Once you have become convinced (between 5-20 minutes of continual chanting), you will find yourself smiling.

If you have a few more minutes, chant to yourself "My dreams have already happened" for a few more minutes while visualizing them in the present.

Then send a thankful message, thanking the higher forces (G-D, the universe, your guardian angels or whatever you believe in) for allowing this creation to have ALREADY MANIFESTED for you. Surround myself with a wonderful feelings of thankfulness.

Continue to smile for a few brief moments and then go back to living your life with the true knowledge that you already have exactly what you wished for.

Try to focus on things that you are grateful for throughout the day.

Then take action with the next opportunity you are given. You may notice that an opportunity will come seemingly from nowhere and very quickly because the belief is there that it has already happened.

Jump onboard the opportunity and continue to be thankful, don't allow fear or "what if's" to enter your mind now.

If you do feel fear, negative thoughts or what if's start to crowl in during the meditation, acknowledge them and set them free. Keep chanting, "It's already happened"

If you happen to remember the negative thoughts that came up during the meditation, write them down, these are your limiting beliefs that you have somehow, somewhere, and sometime ago created and accepted as your own. Go back to Chapter 6, to help you clear these limiting beliefs that are holding you back.

Decide to ignore or replace any limiting beliefs in your consciousness once they are recognized, with positive unlimited thoughts instead. Even if you cannot really do this, and you do find some persistent limiting beliefs creeping up on you, keep going about the process, these thoughts will, with time, slowly disintegrate and become extinct.

Limiting beliefs are not needed any more. Ground and clear limiting beliefs, remove their energy from you by flicking them off with your fingers to the ground near you.

If you do find that a certain day is particularly disturbing and you seem really out of whack, and things are just not going your way, then trying to force yourself to think positively is not going to help. It is just going to make you more frustrated and frustration is not a feeling that gets your desires closer to manifestation. My best recommendation, and one that I use regularly on such days, is taking a nap. Shutting out everything, and when I awaken, things just seem to fall better into place. Sometimes also eating in a nice restaurant also helps. We have more self control when we are not hungry, and visiting a nice restaurant, even on your own, can get you into a better mood.

Remember, what you wanted, you are getting now, the opportunity has arrived,
ACT NOW!
It's yours and you deserve it!
It's yours NOW! In fact, it's already happened!

CHAPTER 9

Rejoice Every Choice Principle #5 for Creating Success, Happiness & Fulfillment

Focus

"You will never reach your destination if you stop and throw stones at every dog that barks"

-Winston Churchill

In this step there is no question to ask yourself, there is only an answer to give yourself:

Now that you have begun taking action and you are believing in the possibility of manifestation of your desire, its time to focus your choices.

Focus means placing your focus on that one thing/Person/Career/Diet/Exercise-Program/System/Method, etc, and follow through with it till the end, until your goal is reached. Focus all of your choices to pinpoint you only in this one direction.

The principle of focus has such a powerful effect that it is difficult to grasp. It is like using a magnifying glass to focus the sun's rays on something. What happens? A fire will start because the sun's energy was focused into one specific point. This is the power of focus.

In a day there are only a certain amount of hours that you can dedicate to achieving your desire, when you focus on one desire at a time, you are putting in 100% of your work potential on that one subject, this focus on the one desire will help it manifest much more quickly than if you were to spread your energies on a few desires at once.

Choose only one desire in each area of life and focus on it with 100% of your focused energy, and in any spare time you have, devote it to enjoying yourself and having fun.

This will help get you aligned with positive energy vibrations that will help good and positive things come to you. Focus on feeling happy, just as you expect your desire to provide you with once it has manifested in your life. This will bring your desires to you much more quickly.

Focusing is, in fact, concentrating energy in one direction, and this concentrated energy is very powerful. Nothing will be able to stop you. Focus allows for persistence until the goal has manifested. By placing your focus on one desire at a time, you may find that you are forming a sort of obsession towards making the desire manifest in your life. This is actually a good thing, it is a positive obsession, focused on the end product of what you do want to have, and not focused on the problems that may be encountered on the way. When your desire becomes your main focus, and all of your energy is going towards its achievement, there is no chance that you will not succeed. The way will often open up before you, slowly but surely, step by step, without you paying too much attention to it. The path will reveal itself to you every time in the form of a new opportunity, and when you are taking focused action and the opportunity arises, you will be ready to take it on, both physically and mentally.

Choosing to focus on one specific goal in each field of your life will allow you focus your thoughts in a way that will provide you with steady persistent and positive thoughts on the subject. This stability in thought is the path to least obstruction on your part towards achieving your desires. You will find the manifestation of your desires will then occur much more readily.

CHAPTER 10

Rejoice Every Choice Principle #6 for Creating Success, Happiness & Fulfillment

Future

"The future starts today, not tomorrow."

- Pope John Paul II

Planning for the future.
The fifth question to ask yourself:
"Will this choice have a positive effect on my future?", "How can I make this choice have a positive effect on my future?"

Every choice you make will affect your future and the future of those close to you. When you consider your choices it is important to consider the consequences your choices will have on your future and the future of those close to you.

Try to choose options that will provide you with pleasure in the future as well as pleasure when manifested. We are motivated by things that are pleasurable, therefore, sometimes we forget to take into account future consequences of our choices when the present holds immense pleasure through the manifestation of our desire.

It is definitely important to consider momentary pleasure, however, it should not be at the expense of future pain. It is best to reconsider the best way to go about achieving your desire with full consideration also of its future consequences on your life. For example, extravagant shopping may be fun at the spur of the moment, however, you *will* have to pay your dues when the time arrives.

On the other hand, if your desire requires you to suffer momentarily it will be more difficult for you to persist with it. When you are suffering, it is very difficult to control your emotions and to remain in a good vibration which allows you to attract positive things into your life more easily. It is best to have balance between current needs and pleasures and future needs and pleasures.

When there is consideration for future events, but there is still some momentary happiness, then your choices are on the right track towards helping you achieve your desires. Your mind will not allow you to immensely suffer in the present for a future prize, especially if the future is considered by your terms as being "far away". If there is some pleasure for the moment as well as promised pleasure for the future in balance then things will flow easier and you will find yourself enjoying the path towards fulfilling your desires as well. This is immensely important because most of the time in life will be spent on the "way" towards achieving your goals and not at their manifestation point itself. Therefore, the "way" must also be fulfilling and joyful for you.

A wonderful and heroic example of making choices that consider a brighter future for yourself and those close to you include what Angelina Jolie, the beautiful Hollywood star, did when she found out that she inherited the BRCA1/2 gene mutation which increased her chances of developing breast cancer to 87% risk and increasing the risk of developing ovarian cancer to a 50% risk. (62) Angelina Jolie, the mother-of-six, choose to act proactively and minimize the risk of developing these cancers as much she could by surgically removing her breasts and ovaries, because she did not want to have her children suffer as she suffered when her mother died at the young age of 56 from ovarian cancer due to this same gene mutation. She placed on the scale the choice of having a long life with her children against her natural beauty and short term health. She took the brave decision and made a choice with the definite consideration of her's and her family's future in mind. (63)

When considering the future while making choices, we must be able to live with our choices now, and in 5 years, in 10 years and even forever.
We must be sure enough with each and every one of our choices as if our life depended on it, because it is the sum of our choices that are the foundation of our life. Our life is a reflection of the sum of our choices.

To Sum Up:

Now that we have covered the Rejoice Every Choice strategy to making successful choices in life, that should be considered before making any decision in life; in the next books in this series, we shall look at some of the most critical areas of your life. We will ask the right questions to guide you and help you know whether your choices are allowing you to be on the right track towards achieving fulfillment, happiness, and success in each of these specific areas of your life.

In the other books in this series we begin to examine your choices in main life areas including:
- Peace of Mind - removal of all forms of anger, fear and guilt feelings
- Health - both physical and mental
- Relationships - both romantic and those with friends and family
- Purpose - your life purpose including your career choice

For each area of your life we will follow the set of tools within the Rejoice Every Choice strategy to making successful choices in life because it is through your choices that you will determine whether you are on the right path towards happily and easily fulfilling your desires or not.

Your choices in each area of life will be examined separately in each of these books. Go to the book covering the area of desire you are wishing to improve in your life to get examples and step by step instructions to making successful choices in life using the Rejoice Every Choice strategy.

Closing Notes

Well, that's it, folks, for Book # 1. I truly hope you now understand the Rejoice Every Choice strategy to making successful choices in life for achieving all of your desires. This approach is simple, doable, practical, and easy to remember.

The questions asked for each principle will help guide you in any and all aspects of your life that you may desire to accomplish or improve. Think of the Rejoice Every Choice strategy outline when you are confronting any new choice in life.

The Rejoice Every Choice strategy for Creating a Successful & Happy Life Series includes:

1. **The Rejoice Every Choice strategy for Creating a Successful & Happy Life:** Book # 1: The Basics Everyone Needs to Know
2. **The Rejoice Every Choice strategy for Creating a Successful & Happy Life:** Book # 2: How to Create Peace of Mind
3. **The Rejoice Every Choice strategy for Creating a Successful & Happy Life:** Book # 3: How to Create Optimum Health

4. **The Rejoice Every Choice strategy for Creating a Successful & Happy Life:** Book # 4: How to Create Great Relationships
5. **The Rejoice Every Choice strategy for Creating a Successful & Happy Life:** Book # 5: How to Create Wealth & Abundance

To summarize the **Rejoice Every Choice Principles**: Think about the value your choice will bring to your life and to those dear to you. Consider your personal love for the choice or desire. Believe, and then Act upon your belief. Stick to your choice by focusing upon it and the actions to achieving it, and always consider the impact this choice will have on yours and your loved one's future.

By following each of the **Rejoice Every Choice Principles** towards making successful choices in life for every decision you wish to accomplish, your life will benefit massively.

Now it's time to show the world the real you: unique, unlimited, all loving and boundless.

I wish you a life of passion and greatness!

With Love,
Galit Goldfarb

BONUS MATERIAL

To supplement the knowledge in this book, I have created an online program titled *"The Magic 8 Step Formula For Success and Happiness – The Online Training Program To Get You Smiling and Passionate About Life Starting Today!"* Go to the link below to get access to this life-altering course:
http://www.theguerrilladiet.com/the-magic-8-step-formula/

This program will introduce you to a special secret step-by-step formula that I personally used to go from having literally nothing to achieving success in all aspects of my life. This course helps you to systematically change your behaviors and belief systems allowing you to go from where you are today to where you truly desire to be just as it did for me.

As my gift to you for purchasing this book, I'm including a 10% off thank you coupon for you as I believe that you really desire to change your current situation, and I would like to help you achieve your goals. This course will help you do it. Here is your coupon code:

6pbookbuyer1

There are only a limited number of discount coupons to this course so please go to the link below to make sure you get your special offer now.

http://www.theguerrilladiet.com/the-magic-8-step-formula/

I invite you to also follow me on:
Facebook: https://www.facebook.com/theguerrilladiet/
Twitter:@GalitGoldfarb
Google Plus: google.com/+GalitGoldfarb
Pinterest: www.pinterest.com/galitgoldfarb
YouTube: https://www.youtube.com/c/Galitgoldfarb
LinkedIn: https://il.linkedin.com/in/galitgoldfarb

In the following index I've included my recommended reading list categorized to help you on your path to specifically changing any aspect of your life in any of your ventures.

INDEX

Recommended Reading List

"I cannot remember the books I've read any more than the meals I have eaten; even so, they have made me."

– Ralph Waldo Emerson

Peace of Mind

The Master Key System – Charles F. Haanel

The Secret – Rhonda Byrne

The Power of your Subconscious Mind – Joseph Murphy

Health

The China Study – Colin T. Campbell

Healthy At 100 – John Robbins

Whole: Rethinking The Science of Nutrition – Colin T. Campbell

Relationships

Emotional Infidelity: How to Affair Proof Your Marriage and 10 Other Secrets To Great Relationships – M. Gary Neuman

What Shamu Taught Me About Life, Love and Marriage – Amy Sutherland

Too Good to Leave, Too Bad To Stay – Mira Kirshenbaum

I Want To Tell You About My Feelings – Mamoru Itoh

Creating Wealth

Think and Grow Rich – Napoleon Hill

Secrets of the Millionaire Mind – T. Harv Eker

Rich Dad Poor Dad – Robert T. Kiyosaki

The Slight Edge – Jeff Olson

You may examine and purchase all of the titles above and more at my online store at:
http://goo.gl/wVLl1X

References:

(1) "Record for best-selling book series". Guinness World Records. Retrieved 18 April 2012.

(2) Salary.Com Personal salary reports and statistics

(3) PARADE magazine NOVEMBER 8, 2013 – 11:37 AM

(4) Wes Moss (2 September 2008). Starting From Scratch: Secrets from 22 Ordinary People Who Made the Entrepreneurial Leap. Kaplan Publishing. pp. 77–86. ISBN 978-1-4277-9828-2. Retrieved 29 January 2013.

(5) Couric, Katie (18 April 2012). "The 100 Most Influential People in the World". *Time*. Retrieved 15 August 2012.

(6) Forbes: "How Sara Blakely of Spanx Turned $5,000 into $1 billion" by Clare O'Connor March 14, 2012

(7) Rose, Lacey (January 29, 2009). "America's Top-Earning Black Stars". *Forbes*. Retrieved May 23, 2012.

(8) 'The Oprah Winfrey Show': Trivia". *Web*. Oprah.com. January 1, 2006. Retrieved June 26, 2012

(9) Miller, Matthew (May 6, 2009). "The Wealthiest Black Americans". *Forbes*. Retrieved August 26, 2010

(10) Biography.com". Biography.com. Retrieved August 26, 2010.

(11) Oprah Winfrey Debuts as First African-American On BusinessWeek's Annual Ranking of 'Americas Top Philanthropists'" (Press release). Urban Mecca. November 19, 2004. Retrieved August 25, 2008.

(12) Nsehe, Mfonobong. "The Black Billionaires 2012". *Forbes*.

(13) Meldrum Henley-on-Klip, Andrew (January 3, 2007). "'Their story is my story' Oprah opens $40m school for South African girls". *The Guardian* (UK). Retrieved March 4, 2007.

(14) "The most influential US liberals: 1–20". *The Daily Telegraph* (London). October 31, 2007. Retrieved May 20, 2010.

(15) Skiba, Katherine (November 20, 2013). "Oprah Winfrey, Ernie Banks awarded Medals of Freedom". *Chicago Tribune*. Retrieved November 20, 2013.

(16) "Oprah Winfrey Receives Honorary Degree at Harvard, Tells Graduates to Max Out Your Humanity | E! Online". Ca.eonline.com. Retrieved 2014-08-22.

(17) Nic Marks, Guardian Professional, Wednesday 30 October 2013 07.00 GMT

(18) Drachman D (2005). "Do we have brain to spare?". *Neurology* 64 (12): 2004–5. doi: 10.1212/01.WNL.0000166914.38327.BB. PMID 15985565

(19) Pascual-Leone, A., Amedi, A., Fregni, F., & Merabet, L. B. (2005). The plastic human brain cortex. *Annual Review of Neuroscience*, 28, 377-401. doi:10.1146/annurev.neuro.27.070203.144216

(20) Rakic, P. (January 2002). "Neurogenesis in adult primate neocortex: an evaluation of the evidence". *Nature Reviews Neuroscience* 3 (1): 65–71. doi:10.1038/nrn700. PMID 11823806.

(21) Chaney, Warren, Workbook for a Dynamic Mind, 2006, Las Vegas, Houghton-Brace Publishing, page 44, ISBN 0-9793392-1-9 [2]

(22) Bos, I; Meeusen, R; Int Panis, L (August 2014). "Physical Activity, Air Pollution and the Brain". *Sports Medicine*.

(23) Doidge, Norman (2007). The Brain That Changes Itself: Stories of Personal Triumph from the frontiers of brain science. New York: Viking. ISBN 978-0-670-03830-5.

(24) The Power of Your Subconscious Mind by Joseph Murphy Ph.D. D.D.

(25) Steven Stosny, Ph.D. How We Make the Same Mistakes Over and Over. Outgrow the habit of turning setbacks into loss and pain into suffering. Psychology Today (2014).

(26) Einstein *Collected Papers*, Vol. 1 (1987, eds. J. Stachel et al.), p. 11

(27) A. Fölsing, *Albert Einstein*, 1997, pp. 36–37.

(28) Einstein, Albert (30 April 1905/January 1906/1956). "A New Determination of Molecular Dimensions". *Investigations on the Theory of the Brownian Movement*. Berne, Switzerland: Dover Publications. ISBN 978-1-60796-285-4. Retrieved 7 August 2013.

(29) "Associate Professor at the Universiy of Zurich und professor in Prague (1909–1912)". *http://www.library.ethz.ch/en/Resources/Digital-library/Einstein-Online* (digital library). Einstein Online (in German and English). Bern, Switzerland: ETH-

Bibliothek Zurich, ETH Zürich, www.ethz.ch. 2014. Retrieved 17 August 2014.

(30) "Professor at the ETH Zurich (1912–1914)". *http://www.library.ethz.ch/en/Resources/Digital-library/Einstein-Online* (digital library). Einstein Online (in German and English). Zurich, Switzerland: ETH-Bibliothek Zurich, ETH Zürich, www.ethz.ch. 2014. Retrieved 17 August 2014.

(31) Evans-Pritchard, Ambrose (29 August 2010). "Obama could kill fossil fuels overnight with a nuclear dash for thorium". *The Daily Telegraph* (London).

(32) Diehl, Sarah J.; Moltz, James Clay. Nuclear Weapons and Nonproliferation: a Reference Handbook, ABC-CLIO (2008) p. 218

(33) "ISRAEL: Einstein Declines". *Time magazine.* 1 December 1952. Retrieved 31 March 2010.

(34) Isaacson, Walter. Einstein: His Life and Universe, Simon & Schuster (2007)

(35) Abraham Lincoln, pp. 55–58. PediaPress

(36) Shenk, Joshua Wolf (October 2005). "Lincoln's Great Depression". The Atlantic. The Atlantic Monthly Group. Archived from the original on 2011-10-20.

(37) Jason Emerson (2012). Giant in the Shadows: The Life of Robert T. Lincoln. SIU Press. p. 420. ISBN 978-0-8093-3055-3.

(38) Abraham Lincoln, p. 17. PediaPress.

(39) wikipedia.org Abraham Lincoln

(40) wikipedia/American Civil War

(41) "Ranking Our Presidents". James Lindgren. November 16, 2000. International World History Project.

(42) "Americans Say Reagan Is the Greatest President". Gallup Inc. February 28, 2011

(43) Harvey J. Irwin, Caroline A. Watt McFarland, An Introduction to Parapsychology, 5th ed. (2011)

(44) Edwin C. May, Sonali Bhatt Marwaha. Anomalous Cognition: Remote Viewing Research and Theory. McFarland, 2014

(45) Jane Henry. Parapsychology: Research on Exceptional Experiences. Psychology Press, 2005

(46) Gennaro Auletta, Giorgio Parisi. Foundations and Interpretation of Quantum Mechanics: In the Light of a Critical-historical Analysis of the Problems and of a Synthesis of the Results. World Scientific, 2001

(47) J.D. Becker, I. Eisele, F.W. Mündemann. Parallelism, Learning, Evolution: Workshop on Evolutionary Models and Strategies, Neubiberg, Germany, March 10-11, 1989. Workshop on Parallel Processing: Logic, Organization, and Technology - WOPPLOT 89, Wildbad Kreuth, Germany, July 24-28, 1989. Proceedings. Springer Science & Business Media, 1991.

(48) Gennaro Auletta, Giorgio Parisi. Foundations and Interpretation of Quantum Mechanics: In the Light of a Critical-historical Analysis of the Problems and of a Synthesis of the Results. World Scientific, 2001

(49) Jeffrey Bub. Interpreting the Quantum World. Cambridge University Press, 1999.

(50) Hans Rickman, M.J. Valtonen. Worlds in Interaction: Small Bodies and Planets of the Solar System: Proceedings of the Meeting "Small Bodies in the Solar System and their Interactions with the Planets". Springer Science & Business Media, 2012.

(51) DEAN RADIN. Experiments Investigating the Influence of Intention on Random and Pseudorandom Events*. Journal of Scientific Exploration. Vol. 3, No. I, pp. 65-79. 1989. Pergamon Press.

(52) Centre for Mindfulness Research and Practice

(53) Train Your Mind, Change Your Brain: How a New Science Reveals Our Extraordinary Potential to Transform Ourselves, S Begley, Ballantine Books, 2007.

(54) Sharon Begley. Scans of Monks' Brains Show Meditation Alters Structure, Functioning. November 5, 2004. The Wall Street Journal.

(55) Time Magazine - How to Get Smarter, One Breath at a Time Scientists find that meditation not only reduces stress but also reshapes the brain, Lisa Takeuchi Cullen Tuesday, Jan. 10, 2006

(56) Wolfram Klapper, Karen Kühne, Kumud K. Singh, Klaus Heidorn, Reza Parwaresch & Guido Krupp (1998). "Longevity of lobsters is linked to ubiquitous telomerase expression". *FEBS Letters* 439 (1−2): 143−146. doi:10.1016/S0014-5793(98)01357-X.

(57) Jacob Silverman. "Is there a 400 pound lobster out there?". howstuffworks.

(58) David Foster Wallace (2005). "Consider the Lobster". *Consider the Lobster and Other Essays*. Little, Brown & Company. ISBN 0-316-15611-6.

(59) How meditation might ward off the effects of ageing,A study at a US Buddhist retreat suggests

eastern relaxation techniques can protect our chromosomes from degenerating, The Observer, Sunday 24 April 2011

(60) Cong YS (2002). "Human Telomerase and It's Regulation". *Microbiology and Molecular Biology Reviews* 66 (3): 407–425. doi:10.1128/MMBR. 66.3.407-425.2002. PMC 120798. PMID 12208997.

(61) A Lutz, LL Greischar, NB Rawlings, M Ricard and RJ Davidson, *Long-term Meditators Self-induce High-amplitude Gamma Synchrony During Mental Practice*, Proceedings of the National Academy of Science, November 16, 2004, volume 101, number 46.

(62) Cancer treatment centres of America Breast Cancer Risk Factors

(63) Angelina Jolie's decision based on BRCA1 test, May 14, 2013

Made in the USA
Middletown, DE
02 January 2019